It is typical of Pastor Tom not to write a self-focused autobiography, but use his rich experiences to help the reader walk closer with Jesus. It is out of that deep abiding relationship that Tom stresses a loving obedience to Jesus' mission to a lost and deeply hurting world.

—Mark Snowden, Director of Missional
Leadership (AMS, DOM),
Cincinnati Area Baptist Association

I have known Tom as pastor and friend for over 10 years now. He has a genuine heart for people everywhere to know the One that loves them more than they know. That message is clear from his Sunday messages to his most recent book, *Through the Door II*. His book will help you effect eternity today not only for you, but for your family and your friends. Good read!

—Lawrence Bergeron,
Executive Director of A Child's Hope Int'l,
author of *Journey to the Fatherless*

What a joy it is to read Tom's daily devotional "Through the Door II: A Worldwide Adventure with Christ." His book focuses on evangelism, but differently than most on the subject. Practical advice and whimsical retelling of his life's events, all add reality to each day's teaching. His wise, concise and to-the-point observations had me reflecting on them for an entire day... and longer. I highly recommend this book for all ages and it would be especially good for those whose families pray and gather for discussion every day.

—David G Hansen, PhD, COL (Ret) USA, author of *In Their Sandals: How His Followers Saw Jesus* and coauthor of *A Visual Guide to Bible Events* and *A Visual Guide to Gospel Events*

THROUGH THE DOOR II

A WORLDWIDE ADVENTURE WITH CHRIST

TOM PENDERGRASS

Published by Author Academy Elite
P.O. Box 43, Powell, OH 43035
www.AuthorAcademyElite.com

Cover Design: Jetlaunch
Interior Design: Jetlaunch
Editor: Alex Farmer

Paperback ISBN: 978-1-64746-624-4

Library of Congress Control Number: 2020923615

For Charles Hailey.
May 10, 1933 – September 17, 2018

A servant missionary who responded to the
call to international missions at the young
age of 70. Your heart for the kingdom was
reflected in your passion for the lost. My life
was blessed to be your pastor and friend.

Each Sunday, I can still see your
hands uplifted in the worship
of our Lord. Until then.

Contents

Foreword

"What is worse than being lost? It is being lost and having no one looking for you"

Pastor Tom Pendergrass

Most of us know the Biblical mandate for missions. We love to hear the stories of people who have gone across the street, or around the world, to share the hope of the Gospel. We have the desire to be involved, however we really don't know how or where to start. If this is you, then this is the

"What is worse than being lost? It is being lost and having no one looking for you"
Pastor Tom Pendergrass

book for you. If you are already serving, then this book is sure to inspire you to attempt even greater things for the Lord!

When I met Pastor Tom Pendergrass in 2010, I knew that this was a man with a passion for Christ and His Kingdom. His enthusiasm for Kingdom advancement was clear and inspiring. The expectation of greater things that the Lord was going to do through simple obedience in the future was evident. As he inspired us with stories of what the Lord had done, I thought to myself, I want to join Him on this wonderful and exciting journey. Several years later, I had the privilege to become part of the team that Pastor Tom leads at Urbancrest, and as the saying goes, the rest is history.

I dreamed of having the opportunity to travel overseas to share the gospel and see people respond. I have since had the privilege to go on many trips and have personal stories to share of what the Lord has done. How about you? Wouldn't you love to have personal stories to share also? We do not need to leave our country to share, though the Lord may give us a wonderful opportunity to go. Sometimes, it is as simple as looking across the table, the street, or work bench to see the opportunities that are in front of us every day.

Join Pastor Tom as he shares stories that will have you laughing and weeping at missional adventures he has been a part of. Be inspired as he guides us through missions as we self-reflect along the way. As you journey through this devotion, don't forget to ask the Lord what He wants you to learn. Listen to how and where He wants you to take action. I look forward to hearing your stories of how the Lord has used you and the amazing adventures that He takes you on.

Andrew Trezona
Missions Pastor, Urbancrest

Introduction:
Writing the Adventure

My wife Donna, six-year-old granddaughter Alianna, and I were traveling on our first worldwide adventure to Perth, Australia. From the United States, Australia is "a fur piece," as we'd say down-home. We've had the privilege to partner with Challenge Newspaper: The Good News Paper, whose ministry headquarters is in Perth.

I was invited not only to meet the Challenge Headquarters team, but to be the keynote speaker for the Keswick Convention (which means "the deeper life"). This took place in both Perth and Esperance, a sea-port city in southwestern Australia. One of my beloved mentors, Dr. Stephen Olford, was a Keswick. I was humbled and honored to be their guest.

It felt like a grand adventure flying by way of Cincinnati, through Los Angeles, Sydney, and finally to Perth, a fifteen-and-a-half-hour flight. One of the attendants told us that halfway through we would have about an hour of "guaranteed turbulence." We were unable to get up, move around, or even use the restroom. Since I've flown through turbulence before, I didn't give her statement much thought. I quickly learned that when someone says "guaranteed turbulence," you should pay attention. Having traveled "down under" twice now, I can truly say that my prayer life is heightened on that leg of the journey.

When we landed in Sydney, I thought to myself that we had "arrived." There was only one more flight before we reached Perth. It couldn't be that bad, especially since we survived the longest, bumpiest flight I had ever experienced. As the pilot came on the speaker, he recited the standard greetings and then drops a bombshell; "Our flying time to Perth is just under five hours." Donna and I looked at each other, completely exhausted. The flight time, including layovers, was thirty-four hours. The airline offered no upgrades or extended leg-room. That's when I realized this was going to be a painful, memorable, portion of our adventure.

As we began our descent, the pilot came on with a few final instructions and a statement that captured my attention. "For those traveling from the USA to Perth, here's a fact that you might find interesting. If we continue to fly over Perth, you would then be heading back towards the USA."

*But you shall receive power when the Holy Spirit has come upon you; and you shall be witnesses to Me in Jerusalem, Judea and Samaria, **and to the end of the Earth**.*

Acts 1:8

That's when this thought raced through my mind; "I have been to the ends of the Earth." Is this what Jesus means in Acts 1:8? Have I somehow completed my part of the Great Commission to "make disciples?" I was overwhelmed as we landed in Perth, realizing that we haven't arrived at our final destination; the worldwide adventure was just the beginning. In the next 30 days, we will look at a journey of adventure into worldwide missions. Here's the exciting news: Our adventure is still being written. Let's take this journey together! My prayer is that you are inspired to accept your role with Christ in missions. Let the worldwide adventure begin!

And Jesus spoke to them, saying, "All authority has been given to Me in heaven and on earth. Go therefore, and make disciples of all nations, baptizing them in the name of the Father and of the Son and of the Holy Spirit, teaching them to observe all things that I have commanded you; and lo, I am with you always even to the end of the age." Amen

Matthew 28:18-20

DAY 1

Jelly, Fudge, and the Great Commission

Every adventure starts somewhere. Mine began in Hamilton, OH. I spent my entire childhood going to church. There was no convincing mom to stay home on Sundays. She ruled as a dictator, never acknowledging democracy in our home.

Mom proudly raised me in the Church of God of Cleveland, Tennessee. Our family's Sunday morning experience was around four and a half hours, followed by a two-hour evening service. We also attended services for two hours on Wednesday evenings and a Saturday night prayer time for two and a half hours. I would listen to great testimonies heralded of how

God changed drug addicts, telling how they gave their lives to Jesus. They were transformed by the power of Christ, and the indwelling presence of the Holy Spirit. It wasn't until my mid-twenties that I realized I also had a drug problem: Mom "drug" me to church every time the door was open.

The Church of God had a women's ministry called the "Willing Workers." This group met on Monday evenings to raise money for missionaries around the world. Six-to-eight ladies gathered to make blankets and clothes. Some were shipped to the missionaries, but the majority of the items were sold. The proceeds were sent to the missionary projects. This is where I began to learn about the Great Commission. The "Willing Workers" made an assortment of pies, cakes, brownies, and cookies, but my Mom's specialty was homemade fudge and grape jelly. I remember hearing the ladies intercede through prayer for our mission-aries, of whom I never had the pleasure of meeting. When the two-hour session was over, my duties began.

On Saturdays, I would fill my red wagon with Mom's fudge and jelly. We would leave home around 9:00 AM and could not return until the wagon was empty. I believe I sold a jar of homemade jelly or fudge to every house in Hamilton, OH. Mom counted the money and prayed that God would multiply, so boys and girls all over the world could hear the name of Jesus and be saved.

On a couple of occasions homeowners asked us to respect the no soliciting sign on the fence. I thought surely that wouldn't apply to raising funds for mis-sionaries. Mom prayed for those homes and that the residents would come to know Christ. I will forever remember those houses that had dogs, mean old "goats," and no soliciting signs.

The Great Commission in my life was not only taught, it was caught.

Mom not only *taught* me Matthew 28:18-20, but she showed me how it was done. I *caught* her heart for missions as we made fudge together and began our walk down Ross Avenue, pulling my red wagon. For every home that purchased fudge or jelly, there was another home receiving the opportunity to hear the Gospel. Mom shared Jesus with neighbors, took prayer requests, and prayed for those needs!

The Great Commission in my life was not only taught, it was caught.

Have you *heard* about missions, or have you *experienced* missions? You need both. When you find your role in missions, invest the remainder of your life experiencing it.

DAY 2

Laundromat Evangelism

I grew up the youngest of four boys. The neighbors might have described the Pendergrass brothers with the same words that Jesus used when describing James and John: "The Sons of Thunder" (Mark 3:17). I look back in amazement of how mom ever survived. My mother had to apologize to every home in a ten-block radius for her boys!

Growing up, I didn't think of us as poor. I remember trying out for Little League Baseball and having someone make fun of my glove and shoes. My glove was a hand-me-down held together by shoestrings. I thought every kid put cardboard in their shoes if they had a hole in them. I went home and asked my mom rather bluntly, "Are we poor?"

Our social status should have dawned on me earlier because of our weekly ritual to the laundromat. Every Saturday, at 6:00 AM, mom would wake me up for laundromat duty to miss the 8 o'clock rush. We didn't get paid for any of our chores. They were taught as responsibilities that gave us the privilege to live in the house, and eat the food served.

This weekly ritual would repeat itself for several years. As a small child, I began to catch on to what mom was teaching about the Great Commission. In seminary, I learned that when Matthew 28:19-20 says "Go," the tensing means "while you're going" or "having gone," make disciples!

Mom taught me that everywhere we went, we were missionaries. She realized that other children were in the same laundromat bondage as I. So, she began bringing coloring pages, craft projects, and Sunday school lessons to build a bridge of love that other kids and their moms could cross to find Jesus.

Look at the word GOD. Stop and circle the first two letters. GO!

Mom also had me practice my Bible memory skills at the laundromat. She would explain to others that kids at church memorize scriptures and recite them on Sundays. She used the laundromat audience to encourage me when I got it right. We didn't have large children programs back then, or all my buddies would have come to church too! If I won the memorization contest, I received a Bible as my prize. She would say, "Tommy, you already have several Bibles and you only need one. Pray about who God would have you give that Bible to." On many occasions, I gave it to a laundromat kid.

To this day, my church rents out a laundromat once-a-month and lets people come to wash and dry their clothes for free. We engage people in everyday life. They share the gospel, pray, cry, and laugh with the folks who come. They set up a TV or a computer and show Christian lessons to the kids, give them prizes, and leave them with hope. Now it is your turn. Find creative ways to share Jesus, and join the adventure!

DAY 3

It's All Greek to Me

For a large part of my life I was incorrectly taught Acts 1:6-8. It is a passage that is still misinterpreted today. It is the launching pad for the Great Commission and a strategy to be joined, not debated. We must make sure we're all on the same page, or we'll never accept our role in the worldwide adventure with Christ.

> *Therefore, when they had come together, they asked Him, saying, "Lord, will You at this time restore the kingdom to Israel?" And He said to them, "It is not for you to know times or seasons which the Father has put in His own authority. But you shall receive power when the Holy Spirit has come upon you; and you shall*

*be witnesses to Me in Jerusalem, and in all Judea and
Samaria, and to the end of the earth."*

Acts 1:6-8

This is the setting for Jesus' ascension into heaven
to be seated at the right hand of the Father, a position of honor and intercession until He returns. The
disciples asked Jesus about the timing of His coming Kingdom and the restoration of Israel. Jesus
rejected any speculation about *times* and *when* He
would come. He shifted the focus to *what* we should
be doing until He comes. During His earthly life,
Jesus denied Himself the knowledge of *when* He
would return (Mark 13:32). John B. Pohill writes in
the New American Commentary that Jesus "depolit-
icized it with the call to a worldwide mission." Even
today we shift the focus from *going* to *learning*. In
other words, we love to study the Book of Revelation
to argue whether we're pre, mid, or post-tribulation.
We forget that if we're pre-trib, Jesus is Coming. If
we're mid-trib, Jesus is Coming. If we're post-trib,
Jesus is Coming. The end result is always that Jesus
is Coming!

*"The story of Jesus led to Jerusalem; the story of the
church led from Jerusalem."*

*John B. Pohill,
The New American Commentary*

Jesus gave the church instructions to be witnesses in Jerusalem, *and* in Judea *and* Samaria, *and* to the end of the earth. I was always taught that you 1) Start in your city 2) Go to your state and the tri-state region, and 3) To the ends of the earth. At starting point one: everyone is responsible. Points two and three: missionaries are responsible.

The church must stop debating about when he is coming and start telling everyone that He is coming!

While training our people to go on international trips, many say that if someone does not go into their own neighborhood, they shouldn't be evangelizing around the world. A little tagline associated with that incorrect way of thinking is: You shouldn't export what you haven't imported. I grew up with the following formula from Acts 1:8.

**Jerusalem
and
Judea & Samaria
and
Ends of the world**

"And," translated from the Greek word **kai**, does not place a priority value of one over another. They are all equally important and necessary. Jesus places an equal value on local, national, and international missions and His missionaries!

DAY 4

Life Changing Faces

Donna and I were raised in the church where our missionary involvement was limited to local missions. Youth leaders had a positive influence on both us, and we soon found ourselves serving as youth volunteers. This is where our adventure in national missions began.

During this time, I read about the Church of God, a home for children in Sevierville, TN. They were in desperate need of volunteer missionaries for a short-term basis. It seemed like a great project to serve others, and pour into our teens the concept of missions outside of our own "Jerusalem."

The church was struggling, and the funding we needed seemed astronomical. The seemingly "closed" door was transportation. We set a goal for raising funds, but we needed a miracle. From my first national trip, I learned that:

When you pray for God to move, it pays to be specific, or He might answer in an unexpected way.

Sevierville, TN is 303 miles from Fairfield, OH. The driving time by car is just four hours and forty-two minutes, unfortunately it's much longer by a yellow school bus. I'm not sure how long it took all thirty-eight of us to get to Sevierville, but it felt like an eternity! I remember when Don Reed called and said that God had provided free transportation. All that we needed to do was pay for the gasoline. I've learned that, "If it sounds too good to be true, it is!" And yet, God answered our non-specific prayer request. He provided a yellow, rust-covered, non-air conditioned, school bus. It was all free, and included a driver, Don Reed himself. Don joked and said the "bus did have air, just with conditions. The condition being you had to open the windows." We opened every one on this sticky July journey.

As I look back on it, I would never attempt to take this trip now. But I was 20 and Donna was 19, so at the time it seemed like a great idea! As we came upon our first incline in the hills of Kentucky, I began to wonder what devil possessed me to think this would work. Certainly, I must have misheard the voice of the Holy Spirit. As it turned out, it would be a life-changing moment for everyone on the trip.

We made it, even though we were exhausted and "starving." It was that evening that I learned not to use that term again. I didn't know anything about being hungry! We unloaded the bus and walked over to the cafeteria to have dinner. As the newbies, every eye was upon us. It would be our last time sitting as a group.

The day we checked in, three siblings also arrived. The oldest girl looked ten, the boy six, and the littlest girl four. As they went through the line and sat down to eat their food, I began to notice that the oldest would break off pieces of her cookie, dinner roll, and fruit to share with her siblings. I alerted the Children's Home Director to what I saw. She spoke to the kids and told them that they were welcome to have seconds. I'll never forget the expressions on those little faces. The two youngest broke out in smiles, and a sense of relief overwhelmed the oldest. It was at that moment I realized how blessed I had been. When God provides a way to go, it will always involve life-changing faces that you'll never forget!

DAY 5

Faith Steps

A frequently asked question is, "If I feel God calling me to the mission field or on a short-term mission project, how do I get started?'"

"Everyone is called...You are either a missionary or a mission field."

J.D. Greear

We're all called, so let's set up a few "baby steps" to expedite the faith process towards missions. In the Christian realm, "baby steps" are often referred to as "faith steps."

Faith Step 1: Work with your local church or denomination to find out what short-term partnerships are available. Many churches team up for short-term mission trips. Passports ensure that you can be a part of any door that God opens.

Faith Step 2: Sign up! Even if you don't know what destination or country God is calling you to, sign up for the next available trip. You're called to go everywhere. Allow the Holy Spirit to flow through you as you seek His call for a particular destination or people group. The bottom line is, you have to start somewhere!

Faith Step 3: If you're traveling internationally, contact your local county health department for that country's required shots. Donna and I have been on every continent in the world except Antarctica, which we (Donna's idea) hope to travel to in 2023. If they require shots, we'll get them. Although, I think it's too cold for a shot to help or for a disease to survive (Donna please read this and reconsider). This faith step isn't designed to scare you, but to prepare you.

> Most people miss out on the worldwide adventure because of a disease commonly known as 'procrastination.'

Faith Step 4: Be prepared to sacrifice and give this worldwide adventure your complete commitment. This will require the sacrifice of time, talent, and treasure. Total dedication will allow several things to happen; 1) You will allow God to stretch you. 2) You will allow God to teach you. 3) You will allow God to be the potter. 4) You will be content being the clay.

Faith Step 5: Attend every session of your missional team training. Come prepared to learn, absorb, and participate in the adventure-building process.

You will build relationships for life and learn how to be flexible. You learn flexibility by experience only. As a part of the training process, you'll talk about being flexible but will never understand it until on the field.

Faith Step 6: Go and serve the needs of the missionaries. Be there to serve, not to set the vision. During your time of debriefing, share with your team insights you learned. This is the proper format to exchange ideas, frustrations, and victories. We are guests in the country or ministry field. Unless you're being asked to do something illegal or immoral, there is usually a reason why a missionary wants things to be done in a certain way. It could be cultural, emotional, or spiritual. The bottom line is, we are servants, not residents.

This list isn't exhaustive, but it is a place to start. It gets you off the sidelines and into the adventure. If health or other emotional issues prevent you from traveling, please know that you can still be an asset to the team. Our process at Urbancrest is simple, and includes this formula:

Pray + Give + Go + Send =
Worldwide Adventure!

DAY 6

When God Calls

I was not prepared when the Lord called me to preach in 1987. I only knew that I was called, and life would never be the same. As I thought about what lay ahead, I had to consider a multitude of ideas, possibilities, and options.

I was thirty, married to Donna (who didn't think she would be married to a preacher), with two children to care for, and a home that I would need to sell in answering the call. I had in my mind that God was going to send me to a foreign land, but I also knew this truth:

The Lord doesn't call the prepared;
He prepares those He calls!

"For you see your calling, brethren, that not many wise according to the flesh, not many mighty, not many noble, are called. But God has chosen the foolish things of the world to put to shame the wise, and God has chosen the weak things of the world to put to shame the things which are mighty; and the base things of the world and the things which are despised God has chosen, and the things which are not, to bring to nothing the things that are, that no flesh should glory in His presence."

1 Corinthians 1:26–29

As I prayed about options, I realized the transition was going to take seven months. I didn't want to waste another moment, so I began researching seminaries that provided distance learning. In 1987, there were

The Lord doesn't call the prepared; He prepares those He calls!

only a handful of seminaries that provided this through cassette tapes, textbooks, and proxied tests.

I attended Moody Bible Institute where the courses would chart the passion and direction of the ministry I was called to. After receiving my courses, I made this commitment. "Lord, these people know what they're doing and I don't have a clue. I'm going to put into practice what I learn."

Three books changed my life: *Successful Soul-Winning* by Dr. Stephen Olford (who would become one of my mentors); *Teaching-With Results* by John Phillips and Herbert E. Klingbell; and *Missions Today, A New Challenge* by Don Hillis.

Successful Soul-Winning taught me that I not only had to share my faith, but had to teach others to share their faith. Dr. Johnny Hunt once said, "If no one else shares their faith, share yours!"

Teaching-With Results said that I needed to study, be prepared, and teach for results. I began using outlines in 1988, at a time when outlines weren't cool.

Missions Today is still directing our ministry. Don Hillis inspired us to adopt the theme of *"It is the duty of the whole church to preach the whole Gospel to the whole world."* Andrew Trezona, our mission's pastor, brought this theme for our branding: The whole church, taking the whole gospel, to the whole world.

DAY 7

A World Missions Conference

I was finishing up my certificate program with the Moody Bible Institute when I began pastoring at the First Baptist Church of Cleves, OH. I will forever be indebted to this small group of people. They took a chance on a thirty-one-year-old dork in a wheelchair.

Here was my impressive resume. I had zero pastoral experience. I'd never performed a wedding, funeral, baptism, or led in the Lord's Supper. I had a two-year bible certificate and had preached a total of seven sermons in front of grown-up people.

I started preaching in August of 1988 and became their pastor that October. My preaching style could be described as zealous without knowledge. I cried more than I preached. I was passionate, and at times, passionately wrong. It was said of the disciple Peter that "the only time he took his foot out of his mouth was to change feet." I identify with that. I was amazed at how God used me during that time to see people come to Jesus and help the church grow. Dr. Rick Warren says it best; *"It is amazing what God will do through a person who doesn't care who gets the credit."*

By the spring of 1989, First Baptist Church of Cleaves was averaging twenty-nine in attendance, including a local cat that occasionally wandered into service. The church had more than doubled, and we decided to hold our first World Missions Conference. When I began pastoring, I didn't personally know any international missionaries. Zip-zero-nada! We baptized 32 my first year at Cleves, and I received notice that we had won 2nd place for baptisms in Cincinnati. Soon I was asked to come to an associational meeting in Norwood, OH. I called my sending church and asked pastor Bob Skirvin what an association even was.

I met three missionaries in the Cincinnati area who became my speakers at the World Missions Conference. The late Bob Dunn was the director, Ed Armitage worked in the prisons, and Larry Gardner served at a feeding center in the over-the-rhine area of downtown Cincinnati. These men made a huge impact on my life!

The strategy for our conference was simple. We had three tables at the front of the worship center, titled Local Missions, National Missions, and Foreign Missions. For each category, we were required to write what we were actively doing in the church. It couldn't be what we wanted or intended to do. We were limited to reality and only allowed to display what our church was effectively doing.

The Book of Acts wasn't called the book of suggestions, good deeds, intentions, long-range plans, or visions of the apostles. It's named the book of Acts because this is what they ACTually did!

Two of the three tables were close to empty. We were involved in a few community outreach projects and gave 10% to the Cooperative Program and 5% to the Cincinnati Baptist Association. But, we did nothing national or internationally. This honest evaluation helped us to repent and to recommit to the Great Commission.

Evaluate your life based on those three categories; local, national, and international. What are you ACTually involved in? What are you ACTually doing? Find a local church's mission conference, and don't miss a day. You will get the opportunity to rub elbows with some of God's finest, servants.

"The most effective method of imparting missionary information is found at the annual missionary conference! An uninformed people will inevitably be an unconcerned people."

Dr. Don Hillis, Missions Today

DAY 8

From the Cornfield to the Community

My oldest daughter, Jessica, has a fear of heights. One summer we went to Stone Mountain in Georgia. If you've never been before, don't let me spoil it for you...but it's a big stone. You can take the tram or if you're a real adventurer, hike to the top. As the tram began to travel upwards, I noticed Jessica seated in the very center staring at the floor. I told her that if the wires broke, she would hit the ground at the same time as those looking out the window. My fatherly advice was to get up, look out your window, and take part in the ride.

Urbancrest was outside the city while still a part of the community. We had to stay intentional about reaching our neighbors. When I first came, we took a "compass" approach, making it a priority to minister to the north, south, east, and west areas of Lebanon.

We identified nine major subdivisions and began making intentional, strategic, and gospel-centered efforts to reach these communities. We used a basic soul-winning approach called People Sharing Jesus. This approach involved the whole church, including small group training. This unified mission endeavor helped us to place a priority on those who weren't at Urbancrest. The vision shifted from the four walls of the church, to the four compass points of our city.

> *"The problem facing the church today is that we're more keepers of the aquarium than we are fishers of men."*
>
> *Dr. E.V. Hill*

People Sharing Jesus had a major tagline, "You never fail when you share Jesus," which helped us to understand the principle of 1 Corinthians 3: 6-8.

> *"I planted, Apollos watered, but God gave the increase. So then neither he who plants is anything, nor he who waters, but God who gives the increase. Now he who plants and he who waters are one, and each one will receive his own reward according to his own labor."*
>
> *1 Corinthians 3: 6–8*

We learned to focus on the process of evangelism and gave equal importance to tilling the ground, planting and watering the seed, and seeing an increase of souls saved. To implement this strategy, we had to convince the church to spend those summer evenings going to the community! These fourteen weeks helped change the DNA of our church regarding local missions.

We met in parks, apartment complexes, cul-de-sacs, Home Depot, Kroger, movie theaters, and Walmart parking lots. No venue was off-limits. We used the movie theater to sponsor Christian movies so we could invite our neigh-bors to attend. We even held special evangelism events during the Warren County Fair (a big deal in our city). VBS, block par-ties, and back-yard bible clubs became routine events during People Sharing Jesus. At every location, we presented the Gospel message and extended the call to life-commitment.

The methods of sharing the Gospel may change, but the message of the Gospel never changes!

Prayer has always been the success of any church evangelism efforts. Before any event, members would go and pray over the community. Everyone was given an assignment, and every adult Sunday school class had to adopt at least one evening outreach. No activities were allowed on our main campus during these fourteen weeks. This fell in line with our mission's vision statement: "the whole church, taking the whole gospel, to the whole world." You don't have to travel around the world to share the Gospel, but you do have to get up and go! Even if it is in your own neighborhood, let the worldwide adventure begin in the place you call home.

DAY 9

Turkey, Three Dogs, and an Open Door!

U rbancrest took their first international trip in 1999 to Istanbul, Turkey. On this trip, I learned how an adventure at home can be as challenging as a day on the mission field.

Donna felt called to go on this trip to Turkey, but I was unable to go as I had to have a painful surgery on my right ankle, leaving me non-weight bearing for twelve weeks. We believed that I could have the operation, and Donna would be able to go on the trip. We prayed and fasted, believing God's timing was right. My surgery was successful, and Donna departed with the team for the next fourteen days to support our IMB missionaries.

I was to rest, recoup, and rehab my ankle, all the while taking care of Donna's three dogs, Maddie, Curly-Sue, and Trouble. The dogs were going down for another afternoon nap as I sat in my recliner to watch golf.

Maddie was a great dane-black lab mix and a large puppy. Curly-Sue and Trouble were brother and sister cocker spaniels. Trouble was asleep near the front door, which I just happened to leave open that afternoon. Curly-Sue was lying near me, and Maddie was sprawled out near the coffee table. We were set up for a perfect storm.

When Trouble was scared, he would immediately hurl whatever was in his stomach. Out of the corner of my eye, I saw someone approaching the house. I started to frantically wave my arms, trying to get her attention before the doorbell rang. At our home, that was a call for revival, dog style. When the doorbell rang, Trouble immediately did a one-and-one half-flip with a half twist in freestyle position and hurled everywhere. Not to get too gross here, but I've never seen that much come out of one small animal! Maddie was next to enter the scene as she stormed towards the front door. She hit the upchuck full speed ahead and collided with Trouble, who was knocked outside onto the porch. Amazingly, the door shut. Maddie proceeded to try to stand up on the door, all the while sliding on Troubles breakfast.

This happened almost like the Rapture will occur "in the moment, in the twinkling of an eye" (1 Corinthians 15:52). I was struggling to get out of the recliner while Trouble was outside on the porch, severely dazed, but okay. As I made my way to the door, I realized my crutches wouldn't navigate well on the hardwood, covered with Trouble's leftovers. I noticed when the lady rang the doorbell, she surveyed what was happening, shook her head, and walked away. To this day, I have no idea what she wanted, but she had seen enough at the Pendergrass looney-tunes inn.

Sometimes a word from home is all a missionary needs to keep going!

After three rolls of paper towels, while crawling on my hands and knees, I cleaned the floors, glass door, and sidelights. I was exhausted and wasn't saying very nice things about Donna's three dogs. As I sat back down, Donna called on the phone. They experienced a very long day on the field and were discouraged. After recalling my eventful afternoon, she laughed uncontrollably and felt encouraged to tackle another day!

The Lord used this trip to Turkey to open numerous doors in the future. Especially, when an earthquake came one evening, and thousands went into eternity. What many believed was an unproductive first trip, was an open door to minister to those in need. Even if life at home is a slippery mess, a word of encouragement can help a missionary persevere despite setbacks on the field.

DAY 10

Niutestamen

Since Urbancrest began our first Global Impact Celebration in 1996, we've had the privilege to partner with some of God's finest servants. Missionaries who sacrifice the comfort and convenience of home to travel where God has called them. As their children graduate high school and return to the States to attend college, they sacrifice the nearness of family relationships. All for a passionate pursuit of their calling to take the gospel to the ends of the earth.

When the church has the vision statement, "The whole church, taking the whole gospel, to the whole world," sometimes that vision reaches places the church has never been. Vanuatu is one of those places. I met Erik and Michele Stapleton at our first mission's conference as they served with the Wycliffe Bible Translators. They shared their calling to go to Vanuatu, and I was amazed by their passion for the Nafe people group to have a Bible in their own language. This was the key to seeing Vanuatu and the surrounding islands come to Jesus.

Each time they shared at our conference, we would receive updates on the New Testament translation process. They shared how many books had been edited, completed, in process, and those still to be translated. It is for the kingdom to ensure each word is accurately translated into Nafe.

You could sense their excitement building, not only in sharing, but in the life of our people who had become prayer partners on their adventure. In 2013, I received one of the first edition prints of the Nafe New Testament with this note inside:

Pastor Tom,

Here is a copy of the Nafe New Testament. I am sending you a copy to say thank you for years of faithful partnership and hoping that when you see it that your hands will be strengthened to support other translation related endeavors in the Lord's harvest field. May the Lord bless you and Urbancrest for your passion and undying commitment to missions and His life-giving gospel.

Erik and Michele Stapleton

Since Niutestamen (New Testament) was released, thousands in Vanuatu and the surrounding islands have said yes to Jesus. The eternal destiny of future generations will continue to be changed forever, passing hope down as a heritage. In my lifetime, I would never have dreamt that our church would be involved in such an endeavor of love for over 17 years. We will spend eternity with brothers and sisters in Christ that we may never have a chance to meet on earth.

> *After these things I looked, and behold, a great multitude which no one could number, of all nations, tribes, peoples, and tongues, standing before the throne and before the Lamb, clothed with white robes, with palm branches in their hands, and crying out with a loud voice, saying, "Salvation belongs to our God who sits on the throne, and to the Lamb!" All the angels stood around the throne and the elders and the four living creatures, and fell on their faces before the throne and worshiped God, saying:*

> *"Amen! Blessing and glory and wisdom,*
> *Thanksgiving and honor and power and might,*
> *Be to our God forever and ever.*
> *Amen."*

> *Revelation 7: 9-12*

Because of the faithful, sacrificial giving of our church, lives are changing around the world. Sometimes we partake in the adventure; other times, we fund it. Either way, it's an adventure worth joining!

DAY 11

Looking Up

Furthermore, when I came to Troas to preach Christ's gospel, and a door was opened to me by the Lord, I had no rest in my spirit, because I did not find Titus my brother; but taking my leave of them, I departed for Macedonia. Now thanks be to God who always leads us in triumph in Christ, and through us diffuses the fragrance of His knowledge in every place. For we are to God the fragrance of Christ among those who are being saved and among those who are perishing. To the one we are the aroma of death leading to death, and to the other the aroma of life leading to life. And who is sufficient for these things? For we are not, as so many, peddling the word of God; but as of sincerity, but as from God, we speak in the sight of God in Christ.

2 Corinthians 2:12-17

The invitation to missions is an unparalleled **blessing** and unequaled **privilege**. But be prepared for discouragement, difficulty, sorrow, and pain. The apostle Paul gives us just a glimpse of what he experienced in his life and adventure with Christ. At Paul's commissioning to ministry from Ananias, he heard the words that would shape his future.

But the Lord said to him, "Go, for he is a chosen vessel of Mine to bear My name before Gentiles, kings, and the children of Israel. For I will show him how many things he must suffer for My name's sake."

Acts 9:15-16

Paul arrives at Troas, a seaport on the Aegean Sea in western Asia-minor. Paul left the riots of Ephesus (preaching Jesus isn't always popular), hoping to meet Titus in Troas and receive an update on the Corinthian believers. Would they repent and do the missionary work assigned to them by God, the Holy Spirit? Corinth was a thriving city that exported goods all over the known world. Paul prayed they would spread the Gospel as well. He was discouraged, felt alone, and as scripture says, "*he had no rest in his spirit.*"

With the riots fresh in his mind, Paul hoped for a positive word from a loyal companion. He passed through Troas before, only to find a barricaded door. The apostle commonly used the metaphor of a door to describe opportunities for kingdom growth. The door that was opened in Troas was a divinely prepared opportunity. Paul was so overwrought and burdened by the situation at Corinth that he found it difficult to focus.

> *For indeed, when we came to Macedonia, our bodies had no rest, but we were troubled on every side. Outside were conflicts, inside were fears. Nevertheless God, who comforts the downcast, comforted us by the coming of Titus, and not only by his coming, but also by the consolation with which he was comforted in you, when he told us of your earnest desire, your mourning, your zeal for me, so that I rejoiced even more.*
>
> *2 Corinthians 7: 5-6*

2 Corinthians 7:5-7 gives us another brief glimpse into what Paul was facing. He was physically exhausted, and his emotional state was summed up with the word "fears." The man God chose to pen two-thirds of the New Testament was afraid. The source of his fear: distractions. In the midst of the distractions, Paul chose to look up. When we decide to get our eyes off distractions and back on God, we unlock all the resources heaven alone can provide. When God showed up He comforted Paul and sent Titus, then Paul received the answer to his prayers. Corinth would live to fight for others, not themselves!

Distractions are focus stealers!

If you're hurting today, choose to look up instead of looking around. The horizontal is temporal; the vertical is eternal. The God, "who comforts the downcast," will comfort you also. What does it take to accomplish the goal to pray, give, go, and send? One word: *focus*.

DAY 12

The Power of Prayer

I t was a typical Sunday morning at the First Baptist Church of Cleves, my first pastoral location. It was there that I fully understood the power of intercessory prayer. The Lord saved this church by increasing in bodies, budgets, and baptisms. We were now close to breaking one hundred in less than two years, with over one hundred baptisms. Little did I realize a storm had been brewing. I was about to get caught in the rip-tide of division.

We had a regularly scheduled business meeting that evening. At my first pastorate, we got together and fought at the business meeting each month. There wasn't much on our monthly agenda. Every meeting, we had the policy to ask if there were any motions from the floor. Very rarely does anything get brought up, and since we were a ministry driven church, the motions generally referred to that particular ministry. But the mic was about to be dropped, temper's flared, and lines drawn in the sand.

A member rose and said, "I think we have enough of *those* people in the church." There was fighting on the outside and fear on the inside. I didn't speak the truth in love. I spoke out of anger, embarrassment, and a little bit of shock that others had agreed with this member. I brought the meeting to an end and asked, "Which one of those people do you think Jesus didn't die for?"

The next morning, I sat down in our family room to write out my resignation letter. While writing this letter, my phone rang. It was my mom calling from Lakeland, FL., fifteen hundred miles away. Mom started the conversation with a question, "Tommy, are you alright?" I lied through my teeth and said I was fine. Mom told me that about an hour ago, the Lord burdened her to pray for me. On her knees, she received a message from the Lord

The moment we've had enough of those people, we need to remember that Jesus gave his life for them.

to tell her son, "Don't quit." Mom abruptly said good-bye and hung up the phone!

My focus and passion changed from horizontal (earthly) to vertical (eternal). Pray for our missionaries. Pray for your pastor and pastoral staff. Pray as if their lives depended upon your prayers, because they do! Mission's ministry begins with prayer. Not just lifeless, non-expectant prayers, but faith-inspired, insistent prayers! Try it and watch God move. Keep praying for our missionaries. Send them an email, a card, or better yet, make plans to visit them in the field.

DAY 13

A Basket of Hope

I was sitting at home watching the evening news, when a reporter stated that they would be back with a great message of hope from a church impacting their community. This caught my attention since it's not the norm to get great, prime-time, TV coverage of a church doing ministry.

In Springdale, Arkansas, the news spoke of a church that was impacting their community through a program known as "Baskets of Hope." I knew this event would be highly evangelistic in its approach. At Thanksgiving, this church was helping five thousand families with a Basket of Hope. The church welcomed the entire family to come for special activities for the kids, while teens and parents heard a message of hope. The reporter interviewed a few of the folks who received baskets. It was all positive, seemingly unedited, and inspiring.

The segment finished and my wheels started spinning. When I contacted the church, they were ecstatic that we would be intentional about not only giving a basket of hope, but sharing the hope found in Jesus Christ. I began calculating what it would take to start up a ministry effort like this and settled on the figure of $10,000. Now I ask myself, why do we always dream so small?

I cast the vision to our mission pastors. The basic ministry is to invite families to come to evening service and leave with a first-class basket of food for Easter, Thanksgiving, and Christmas. At the time, we didn't have that $10,000, but we prayed together and asked God to supply the resources and the laborers. We were available and willing to move forward by faith.

About an hour later, I received a phone call from a mission partner and friend who said, "I'm heading your way now. I've been given a large grant that I can give away to a church, but the money has to go to feed people. I'm bringing you a check for $10,000." For the next three years, this ministry would be funded with a $10,000 check per year. In twenty-four hours, God planted the vision in our hearts and provided the funds for the next three years. Today, that ministry is self-funded by those who've been blessed to serve in this capacity. We've also seen close to two hundred professions of faith in Jesus Christ. Thanksgiving 2019, we did an entire banquet for the families of our community. A single mom with five children told me it was the first time in nine months they had been out to dinner anywhere. God answers prayer!

> *Now to Him who is able to do exceedingly abundantly above all that we ask or think, according to the power that works in us, to Him be glory in the church by Christ Jesus to all generations, forever and ever. Amen.*
>
> *Ephesians 3:20*

The past few weeks, Andrew, our mission pastor, and I have been praying and seeking the Lord about how we could impact our community during the Covid 19 pandemic. When you pray for God to move and are willing to be available, get ready for a miracle!

Our church was contacted by a missionary friend asking if we would be interested in having a free semi-trailer fully loaded with fresh food. An initiative called Farmers for Families, working with President Trump during the Covid 19 pandemic was not only helping farmers, but families. They'll deliver one thousand-thirty 30lb boxes each week to the church parking lot for free! No restrictions on what we can give away or share. Andrew and I prayed for God to provide for our city and God answered. It's not too late to get in on the action. Start praying, start expecting, and be ready to work.

DAY 14

The Festival of Trumpets

Donna and I, along with Larry and Sylvia Randolph, were privileged to travel to Africa. We worked with missionaries from the International Mission Board, Tim and Louise Shuppe in Yaounde, Cameroon. Yaounde is a bustling city of over one million people open to the gospel.

I'll never forget Larry saying that he wasn't called to go to Africa, but he did feel called to go along and pray.

Tim met us at the airport, hugged my neck, and cried. He told me how many healthy people he had asked to minister in Cameroon. They refused to come because of the stigma of Africa. He was blown away that we came, and has since used our story to inspire others.

At the end of our two-week adventure, we had t-shirts printed that said, "I survived Tim Shuppe's driving!" When he was driving, I confessed sins I hadn't even committed because I thought for sure we were going home to meet Jesus. Tim drove with passion, zeal, and reckless abandon. Cameroon is a French governed nation and is famous for its no-lane, no-rules, roundabouts. For my American friends, the best way I can describe it is by picturing a demolition derby. That is a small dose of Yaounde.

I walked through crocodile-infested rivers, saw thousands of bats that were bigger than bald eagles, and had a witchdoctor sacrificing chickens and casting spells on me. We checked in the day before our departure to verify our flight infor- **Stepping up doesn't mean that you are without fear, it means you are trusting God to deliver despite your fear.** mation, only to arrive at the airport the next day to be told that our flight doesn't exist. I think Donna and I had collected about 100 prayer partners. It wasn't enough!

The Festival of Trumpets is a musical celebration that began around 6:00 and continued long into the night. Ube University (a Presbyterian college) was the featured group, and the word amazing doesn't justly describe how good they were. All those who were a part of the musical celebration were called up for the finale, "When the Saints Go Marching In." They sang a couple of choruses before Tim announced that we were leaving. He later said that they'd be singing that song until 1:00 AM, and he wasn't joking!

It was during intermission that I was given ten minutes to speak. That's right, ten whole minutes, with an interpreter. During the first musical section, I became very restless about the message the Lord challenged me to speak. It was a great, although brief sermon, that I've never used. During the first section, the Holy Spirit impressed upon me to speak on hell. After a short argument with God, I leaned over and told Larry to pray. Pray that I hadn't missed the message and that I had a great interpreter. My interpreter, a young, college-aged student, was very dynamic and expressive.

You could have heard a pin drop during my message on hell. I noticed a young man walking back and forth behind the Ube University choir. He was very respectful and seemed to be praying over them. I gave the invitation to say yes to Christ and seven of the choir members were the first to respond. The gentleman in the back of the room was their new chaplain. He had prayed all day that someone would share the gospel because he knew many in the choir were lost. His prayers were answered. Do you need to pray right now and ask Jesus to forgive you of your sins and to save you from hell? Don't delay!

DAY 15

Changing Prayer

I am frequently asked, "How does God speak to people today?" I think a better question could be, "How do I listen to God in a world full of distractions?" The answer to both questions is surprisingly simple. God communicates with His people through the Holy Spirit, His Word, people, and circumstances.

The Holy Spirit is the third person of the Godhead. He comes to live in your life the moment you trust in Jesus Christ as Lord and Savior. The Holy Spirit is a gift from God that will never leave you nor forsake you. Even the fruit produced in life is said to be the fruit of the Spirit, which will guide, comfort, and correct us on our journey. The Holy Spirit sanctifies us, to be used as vessels of honor. It is the Holy Spirit that convicts the heart, cleanses us for service, and calls us to our missional adventure.

If we confess our sins, He is faithful and just to forgive us our sins and to cleanse us from all unrighteousness.

1 John 1:9

God's word is used to teach us about our biblical responsibility to advance God's Kingdom on earth. Jesus prayed for His Kingdom to come, and one day that prayer will be answered. Until then, we find out what our role is, and we perfect that role.

Your word is a lamp to my feet
And a light to my path.

Psalm 119:105

God uses ordinary people, filled with the Holy Spirit, to speak a word of encouragement and edification. He is available to everyone that seeks to grow in Christ and work for the kingdom. I want to encourage you to pray for the Lord to place people into your life that see the potential inside you. People can influence you to grow closer to Jesus.

The Lord has used circumstances in my life, both joyful and painful, to shape and mold me into the man of God He desired me to be. When David cried, "thy rod and thy staff comfort me," (Psalm 23:4) I can relate. There are times the Good Shepherd has to gather His wandering, strong-willed sheep. Circumstances draw our attention, to remind us of the preciousness and brevity of life.

Listen to God and how He wants to change our prayer life. I'm not talking about being guilted into praying more. It's about changing the wording, tone, and attitude of our prayers.

We change the wording of our prayer to make it biblical. Not if you want us to go, but when should we go. God's word has already commissioned and called us to go the day we give our lives to Jesus. When Isaiah heard the call of God, he did not hesitate when he spoke.

The tone and attitude of prayers change from accusatory to exploratory. We move from the recipient to the giver. Our attitude as a servant places us in a position to hear from God. We must obey what is heard and not debate. Many times, we miss out on the adventure God has planned because we are looking for a miracle. He wants us to be the miracle through us. Allow the Holy Spirit, His Word, His people, and His circumstances to bless and shape your life.

> Also I heard the voice of the Lord, saying:
> "Whom shall I send,
> And who will go for Us?"
> Then I said, "Here am I!
> Send me."
> Isaiah 6:8

DAY 16

Missions & You

My favorite week at Urbancrest is during our Global Impact Celebration, the annual missions conference. We allow scripture to set the purpose of the church. The biblical basis for this emphasis on missions comes from the book of Acts.

> From there they sailed to Antioch, where they had been commended to the grace of God for the work which they had completed. Now when they had come and gathered the church together, they reported all that God had done with them, and that He had opened the door of faith to the Gentiles.
>
> *Acts 14:26-27*

The church at Antioch commissioned Paul and Barnabas to share the gospel. Upon the completion of Paul's first missionary journey, they returned to Antioch to report all that God had done.

I have asked our people to describe the annual mission conference in bullet form phrases. Here is a sampling of their thoughts.

Missions on steroids!
Drinking missions from a fire hose!
The missional influence on our children!

All three of which are true. The first goal of our annual conference is designed so the church can rub shoulders with some of God's finest servants on this planet. There are countless church members who have never had any correspondence with a missionary.

Sign up to pray and intercede for missionaries. They'll send you monthly or quarterly prayer requests and newsletter updates. Remember their birthdays and anniversaries. Pray for them and their children.

Make the missions conference a "holy" week for you and your family. Plant the seeds of missions into your children while they are young. Your preschoolers, children, and teens will learn, grow, and find out their kingdom assignment. Every session has a different focus where you'll be encouraged to pray, give, go, and help send missionaries around the world.

To follow God's mission is to make missions a part of your spiritual DNA.

Another emphasis is to minister, serve, and refresh our missionaries while they're here. We've had numerous missionaries attend and share that they were spiritually burned out, discouraged, and ready to quit until they came to this conference. They were greatly encouraged by the number of people who treated them with love, respect, and a servant's heart.

Another benefit is the networking that goes on behind the scenes. Watching missionaries minister and lift each other in prayer leaves me in awe of the moving of the Holy Spirit. The Lord may call you to pray. He may require you to invest in His kingdom. He may invite you to go on a short-term project. He will certainly ask you to join in the adventure!

DAY 17

Your Eternal Investment Portfolio

H ave you ever thought of giving as an eternal investment? For one widow, giving became an adventure of faith. Instead of keeping what she had, she chose to share it with a stranger.

> *Then the word of the Lord came to him, saying, "Arise, go to Zarephath, which belongs to Sidon, and dwell there. See, I have commanded a widow there to provide for you." So he arose and went to Zarephath. And when he came to the gate of the city, indeed a widow was there gathering sticks. And he called to her and said, "Please bring me a little water in a cup, that I*

may drink." And as she was going to get it, he called to her and said, "Please bring me a morsel of bread in your hand."

So she said, "As the Lord your God lives, I do not have bread, only a handful of flour in a bin, and a little oil in a jar; and see, I am gathering a couple of sticks that I may go in and prepare it for myself and my son, that we may eat it, and die."

And Elijah said to her, "Do not fear; go and do as you have said, but make me a small cake from it first, and bring it to me; and afterward make some for yourself and your son. For thus says the Lord God of Israel: 'The bin of flour shall not be used up, nor shall the jar of oil run dry, until the day the Lord sends rain on the earth.'"

So she went away and did according to the word of Elijah; and she and he and her household ate for many days. The bin of flour was not used up, nor did the jar of oil run dry, according to the word of the Lord which He spoke by Elijah.

1 Kings 17:8-16

Urbancrest stretches our people to give sacrificially to a "Faith Promise Fund." A "Faith Promise" is simply a promise made by faith. It implies that I'm now giving out of my reserve and I don't have any natural means to replenish it. I'm trusting the Lord to take care of my family.

The Bible tells stories of God teaching people to trust Him for their future needs in unusual ways. The

Lord instructed Elijah to go to Zarephath, a place of refining. He met Elijah's needs right in the middle of enemy territory. Elijah proclaimed a fast that would last for three years as he hid out at the Brook Cherith and ate food that the ravens brought. It sounds like he had already been to the place of refining, but God was just getting started. With an ironic twist, the judgment Elijah passed on to Ahab and Jezebel when the Brook Cherith dried up. Has God ever allowed a brook to dry up in your life so that He might stretch you?

The Bible says that God had already commanded the widow to provide for Elijah. Elijah obeyed the Lord and got an ear full from this woman. Both Elijah and the widow were dependent on the Lord and had to trust Him with their future. They experienced a

Has God ever allowed a brook to dry up in your life so that He might stretch you?

miracle through exercising their faith by giving up their reserves to receive an unlimited supply from the Lord. The Faith Promise is an invitation to increase your eternal portfolio.

Today's trust is tomorrow's victory!

Paul Gotthardt

DAY 18

A Faith Promise

"Is a Faith Promise something that I pray about and ask God to allow to flow through me?"That was a question posed to me by a new family visiting our church. Yes, the Lord invites you to enter into the arena of sacrificial giving. Many are invited; few accept the challenge.

Now as He was going out on the road, one came running, knelt before Him, and asked Him, "Good Teacher, what shall I do that I may inherit eternal life?"

So Jesus said to him, "Why do you call Me good? No one is good but One, that is, God.

You know the commandments: 'Do not commit adultery,' 'Do not murder,' 'Do not steal,' 'Do not bear false witness,' 'Do not defraud,' 'Honor your father and your mother.' "

And he answered and said to Him, "Teacher, all these things I have kept from my youth."

Then Jesus, looking at him, loved him, and said to him, "One thing you lack: Go your way, sell whatever you have and give to the poor, and you will have treasure in heaven; and come, take up the cross, and follow Me." But he was sad at this word, and went away sorrowful, for he had great possessions.

Mark 10:17-22

Jesus counsels a rich, young ruler to sell everything, give it to the poor, invest in an eternal portfolio, die to self, and follow Him. Jesus invites a man who is young, healthy, and wealthy, but empty. He came to Jesus wanting a behavioral modification. What is necessary to inherit eternal life? His self-righteousness was found in keeping a to-do list, yet he knew there was more. He wasn't expecting the challenge, for treasure had become his idol. He knew the scriptures began with, "You shall have no other gods before Me," yet his treasure stood between him and His master's call.

If you break the first commandment you break them all!

Martin Luther

Jesus' invitation wasn't to lose it all, but to gain it all! What the rich, young ruler needed was not another behavior modification course, but a life-changing, radical experience with Jesus Christ. He left without having his life transformed or his eternal destiny sealed.

A Faith Promise Commitment places no financial barriers before our commitment to Christ and His kingdom. Jesus said, "if you do it to the least of these, you've done it to Me. I was hungry and you gave me bread!" (Matthew 25:40) Do you feel Jesus was rough on this man? If asked you for advice, what would you have told him? Would you say, "Sell it now! Don't pass up this adventure for a few toys and a seemingly secure portfolio! Give to the poor!" If you hesitated, it might be because you have never surrendered your finances to Jesus. The Faith Promise Commitment is a launching pad for sacrificially giving. It helps you break the 10% idol that many hold dear and allows missional giving to begin!

DAY 19

Unexpected Giving

And behold, a certain lawyer stood up and tested Him, saying, "Teacher, what shall I do to inherit eternal life?"

He said to him, "What is written in the law? What is your reading of it?"

*So he answered and said, "You shall love the **Lord** your God with all your heart, with all your soul, with all your strength, and with all your mind," and "your neighbor as yourself."*

And He said to him, "You have answered rightly; do this and you will live."

But he, wanting to justify himself, said to Jesus, "And who is my neighbor?"

Then Jesus answered and said: "A certain man went down from Jerusalem to Jericho, and fell among thieves, who stripped him of his clothing, wounded him, and departed, leaving him half dead. Now by chance a certain priest came down that road. And when he saw him, he passed by on the other side. Likewise a Levite, when he arrived at the place, came and looked, and passed by on the other side. But a certain Samaritan, as he journeyed, came where he was. And when he saw him, he had compassion. So he went to him and bandaged his wounds, pouring on oil and wine; and he set him on his own animal, brought him to an inn, and took care of him. On the next day, when he departed, he took out two denarii, gave them to the innkeeper, and said to him, 'Take care of him; and whatever more you spend, when I come again, I will repay you. So which of these three do you think was neighbor to him who fell among the thieves?' And he said, 'He who showed mercy on him.'

Then Jesus said to him, 'Go and do likewise.'"

Luke 10:25-37

There are three categories of people in life: Takers, Keepers, and Givers.

Takers have the philosophy of "What's yours is mine, and I'm going to take it." The thieves had an entitlement mindset of I deserve this, and you don't.

It's a survival of the fittest approach that is rampant in society.

Keepers are depicted by the priest and the Levite in this story. When they both approached the man lying half-dead on the side of the road, they took a step to one side and continued on their journey. The heart of a keeper is "What's mine is mine, and I'm going to keep it."

Then there are the givers in life, represented by the Good Samaritan. The mindset of a giver says, "What's mine is yours, and I'm going to give it." This attitude says, I could be that traveler on the side of the road. I'm going to not only give, but get personally involved in his life.

> *But this I say: He who sows sparingly will also reap sparingly, and he who sows bountifully will also reap bountifully. So let each one give as he purposes in his heart, not grudgingly or of necessity; for God loves a cheerful giver.*
>
> *2 Corinthians 9:6–7*

As we ask people to pray about what they're sacrificial gift will be, it echoes the words of Jesus. "Go and do likewise." It's a challenge to be personally involved in a monetary way as a declaration of responsibility. The question is, will I pray and ask the Lord what He wants me to do? Will I listen and respond by faith?

DAY 20

Let's Go

Our worship pastor uses the phrase, "Let's Go" as he invites people to passionately engage in worship. In a worship service at Philippi, an opportunity arose for a short-term mission trip. The church at Philippi had supported Paul since he founded the church, and were sending aid to the jailed apostle. Under the Roman system, families were the primary source of feeding a prisoner.

The announcement asked for a volunteer to go to Rome, about a three-month journey. Epaphroditus said, "Here am I send Me!" Many have called this the first time a church member went on a short-term mission trip.

Yet I considered it necessary to send to you Epaphro-
ditus, my brother, fellow worker, and fellow soldier,
but your messenger and the one who ministered to my
need; since he was longing for you all, and was dis-
tressed because you had heard that he was sick. For
indeed he was sick almost unto death; but God had
mercy on him, and not only on him but on me also,
lest I should have sorrow upon sorrow. Therefore I sent
him more eagerly, that when you see him again you
may rejoice, and I may be less sorrowful. Receive him
therefore in the Lord with all gladness, and hold such
men in esteem; because for the work of Christ he came
close to death, not regarding his life, to supply what
was lacking in your service toward me.

Philippians 2: 25-30

I would think Epaphroditus began his adventure as anyone going on their first short-term mission trip. But somewhere on the journey, things took a turn for the worse. He became ill and nearly died. As a pastor, I've joked about how we consider it a successful short-term trip when "they all come back alive." I had a conversation with one of our missionaries who sent a medical team into a volatile situation. Two team members were martyred for the name of Jesus. Seeing the pain in his countenance, I realized he understood when Paul said if Epaphroditus had passed, it would have added "sorrow upon sorrow." Thank God this story has a happy ending, but reality happens, and life can change instantly.

Paul said to hold those who go in high esteem. Going always involves risks, but the kingdom has no

other strategy! Epaphroditus felt that he had failed
his commissioning, and it was the church of Rome
that ministered to him. He was sent to minister and
needed to have others attend to him. Paul said his
illness was because of His work for Christ.

> *Nevertheless you have done well that you shared in my
> distress. Now you Philippians know also that in the
> beginning of the gospel, when I departed from Mace-
> donia, no church shared with me concerning giving
> and receiving but you only. For even in Thessalonica
> you sent aid once and again for my necessities. Not
> that I seek the gift, but I seek the fruit that abounds to
> your account. Indeed I have all and abound. I am full,
> having received from Epaphroditus the things sent
> from you, a sweet-smelling aroma, an acceptable sac-
> rifice, well pleasing to God. And my God shall supply
> all your need according to His riches in glory by Christ
> Jesus. Now to our God and Father be glory forever and
> ever. Amen.*

Philippians 4:14-20

Paul wanted to emphasize one point. The
Philippians would see fruit deposited into their eternal portfolios. When we pray, give, and go, we will
receive fruit for our investment of time, talent, and
resources.

> *"Not that I seek the gift, but I seek the fruit that
> abounds to your account."*

Philippians 4:17

DAY 21

My Burning Bush

Now Moses was tending the flock of Jethro, his father-in-law, the priest of Midian. And he led the flock to the back of the desert, and came to Horeb, the mountain of God. And the Angel of the Lord appeared to him in a flame of fire from the midst of a bush. So he looked, and behold, the bush was burning with fire, but the bush was not consumed. Then Moses said, "I will now turn aside and see this great sight, why the bush does not burn."

Exodus 3:1-3

Moses' calling to be a missionary to Israel is one of the most beloved callings and debates ever recorded for man. God gives a burning bush phenomenon to get Moses' attention on the back-side of a Midian desert. Moses, intrigued by the sight, drew near to see "why the bush does not burn."

Moses was going about his daily routines as a shepherd when God interrupted to invite him on a journey. As Moses came near to the burning bush, God called out and told him that his life would never be the same. Moses was instructed to take his shoes off for God's invitation to join Him on the missional "holy ground." When we have an encounter with God at our "burning bush," settling for a routine life of our choice is not an option.

Let me take you to the side of Interstate Four, just outside Tampa, Florida, where I had my "burning bush" encounter with God. A car came across the median, hitting us head on, resulting in a five car, one semi pile up. I was lying on the floorboard of my car, trying to figure out what had just happened. My world was spinning in slow motion. I knew the routine in my life was irreversibly altered. When the Lord spoke to my heart and said, "Tom, if you'll trust Me, I'll use you," I had no idea where He would take me. I have now been to five continents to preach the Gospel.

My return to Christ as a prodigal happened in the fall of 1986 at North Fairfield Baptist Church. After four and a half years of running from God, I found Him at a baptism service as I watched a seven-year-old boy go through the waters. The Holy Spirit spoke to my heart, reminding me that this was what His kingdom is all about. As a prodigal, I had my eyes on things, myself, and people instead of Jesus Christ! Through my burning bush, I saw the death, burial, and resurrection of Jesus through baptism.

I rededicated my life to Christ that evening and thought I would go back to my previous Christian walk. Little did I know the surprises He had in store for my life. If I had known what lay ahead, I would not have believed it. I would have tried to bargain with God, just like Moses did in Exodus 3.

When the Lord gives you a burning bush moment, make the most of it. Any sacrifice He asks you to make in "going" adds to your eternal portfolio in Heaven. If He asks you to join His adventure through praying, giving or going, it will be the most exciting experience of your life since your salvation. See His hand at work with your own eyes!

DAY 22

Mission Possible

*Go therefore and make disciples of all the nations,
baptizing them in the name of the Father and of the
Son and of the Holy Spirit, teaching them to observe
all things that I have commanded you; and lo, I am
with you always, even to the end of the age. Amen.*

Matthew 28:19-20

Have you thought about joining the challenge of
Matthew 28:19-20 to "Go?" Your adventure could
take you to your cul-de-sac, city, state, or nation.
It may also take you to the four corners of the earth.
The issue is not the where, when, or why, but "Who" is
inviting you on the journey. We have a built-in GPS,

better known as the Holy Spirit. It is the Holy Spirit who disturbs our mind and heart for a particular family, people group, or geographical location.

A short-term trip at Urbancrest usually runs from seven to seventeen days in length. When you respond to the call, a process will take place as you prepare for the adventure.

1. Attend the informational trip meeting to hear about the available trips or a particular trip you feel called to go on.

2. If it is an international trip, a passport must be secured. Required vaccines will need to be administered as your first step of faith.

3. Pray about which project God is calling you to and begin to assemble a prayer team with a minimum of 25 committed prayer warriors who will intercede for you each day.

4. Sign up and clear your schedule to attend every team meeting. Fill out required paperwork, including your testimony to salvation and why you want to be a part of the team.

5. Cultivate a servant's heart and attitude. You know you have this when you are treated like a servant, and it does not bother you. Commit to going as a servant of Jesus Christ.

6. Own the responsibility of ministering to the missionaries you will work with. We are not there to cast vision, but to join it.

7. Learn your role on the team and commit to pray for your team members.

8. The keyword used for every trip we commit to is this: Flexible! Be flexible as things change daily on His adventure. He opens doors and orchestrates events and circumstances beyond our control. We adapt as the Spirit moves. We adjust as the enemy confronts. We remain available in humility, mercy, and grace.

Having led multiple youth, short-term trips (it's always an experience with teens), my goal is to mentor Christ to the team and to see them take ownership. Our trips to Buffalo, Philadelphia, Baltimore, Chicago, New York City, and most recently Las Vegas have produced numerous young people who continue to go on mission trips through college and beyond. Several team leaders for our trips started in our youth department and now lead trips around the world!

As opportunities arise, use the gift of discernment with this frame of mind. Lord, not *if* you want me to go, but *where*. You may join your church locally in reaching out to the community. When we invest our lives in others with a humble, servant heart, missions become multigenerational, and the Kingdom is advanced! The next time the Holy Spirit gives an opportunity, find your role in the adventure, and join the celebration!

DAY 23

Eyewitness

For we did not follow cunningly devised fables when we made known to you the power and coming of our Lord Jesus Christ, but were eyewitnesses of His majesty.

2 Peter 1:16

Seeing is believing! Peter records for our benefit and faith that he was an "eyewitness to His majesty." Peter wasn't communicating second-hand accounts, exaggerating to make a point, or relying upon the eyewitnesses of others when it came to Jesus Christ being the Messiah and soon coming King. Peter saw it with his own eyes, and added one more detail so we can grasp who Jesus is.

Now after six days Jesus took Peter, James, and John his brother, led them up on a high mountain by themselves; and He was transfigured before them. His face shone like the sun, and His clothes became as white as the light. And behold, Moses and Elijah appeared to them, talking with Him. Then Peter answered and said to Jesus, "Lord, it is good for us to be here; if You wish, let us make here three tabernacles: one for You, one for Moses, and one for Elijah."

While he was still speaking, behold, a bright cloud overshadowed them; and suddenly a voice came out of the cloud, saying, "This is My beloved Son, in whom I am well pleased. Hear Him!" And when the disciples heard it, they fell on their faces and were greatly afraid. But Jesus came and touched them and said, "Arise, and do not be afraid." When they had lifted up their eyes, they saw no one but Jesus only.

Matthew 17:1-8

Peter reminds us that the Majesty they saw was supernatural, for He was endorsed by God Himself. We not only saw His majesty, but we also heard the voice of the Father. He saw Moses and Elijah and became so caught up in the moment that he wanted to build a tabernacle for all three!

As I thought about that mountain for Peter, James, and John, it dawned on me that many people only hear the stories of the mission field. As adventurers give testimony to what they saw, heard, and accomplished, the majority in the church are listeners as people report what God had done through them. They weren't participants. They weren't even spectators, but hearers of what God has done. Some prayed for the team, and some gave so they could travel. But, the rest were listeners.

On one recent trip to Las Vegas, our team had a "holy mountain" encounter with God. We came off the expressway in Old North, Las Vegas, and entered "Tent City," one of the largest gatherings of homeless in the USA. Conversations ended, and prayers filled our van! Here are a few of the realities I experienced through their prayers.

"I have never known what it was like not to have a home."

"I've never experienced a lack of air-conditioning or heat."

"I've never gone without a meal in my life."

I listened as several young men had an encounter with the Holy Spirit. I heard prayers of gratitude for how they were blessed. I also heard them pray from the heart for "Tent City." They were eyewitnesses to the sights and the sounds of those in need. They were no longer spectators but participants. That's the power of going!

DAY 24

The Greatest Obstacle

Over my thirty years as a pastor, I've heard a lot of reasons why people "can't" go! From some real whopper of excuses to direct responses.

> *But you shall receive power when the Holy Spirit has come upon you; and you shall be witnesses to Me in Jerusalem, and in all Judea and Samaria, and to the end of the earth.*
>
> *Acts 1:8*

Since the outpouring of the Holy Spirit, we have been empowered to go. Just like Moses, Jonah, the apostle Peter, and this pastor, we tend to run. I was fourteen years old when I first felt the Holy Spirit move in my heart that I was to be a pastor. I remember when our pastor said that we need to pray for more young men to respond to the call. I leaned over to a buddy and said jokingly, "Who would want that job?" Sixteen years later, I would say yes.

Many in the church describe their encounter with the Holy Spirit as a calling which can sit dormant for a little while, or fourteen years in my case. My greatest obstacle as a teen was sports. My schedule and priorities were set. Today, I hear it explained in terms of career, education, searching for a spouse, or it's not the right "season of life." We're not the first to make those excuses. In essence, my present day circumstances, commitments, and responsibilities have to be addressed before I can follow.

> *Now it happened as they journeyed on the road, that someone said to Him, "Lord, I will follow You wherever You go."*
>
> *And Jesus said to him, "Foxes have holes and birds of the air have nests, but the Son of Man has nowhere to lay His head."*
>
> *Then He said to another, "Follow Me."*
>
> *But he said, "Lord, let me first go and bury my father."*
>
> *Jesus said to him, "Let the dead bury their own dead, but you go and preach the kingdom of God."*
>
> *And another also said, "Lord, I will follow You, but let me first go and bid them farewell who are at my house."*

But Jesus said to him, "No one, having put his hand to the plow, and looking back, is fit for the kingdom of God."

Luke 9:57-62

For some, it's not their present, but their past. This can be spoken in true humility or from a spirit that has been deceived by the evil one. Jesus refers to a past that's forgiven in terms of grace; Satan refers to it as guilt! When God calls you to join His adventure, He will take your past to change the future of someone bound in sin. No matter what you have done, He will recommission your transformed life for His glory and honor.

DAY 25

Carpe Diem

In 1989, a movie entitled *Dead Poets Society* took Hollywood by storm. The movie centers around an all-boys school for higher learning, where only the best are accepted, and tradition is strong and time-honored. Conformity to tradition is required, and punishment is without mercy for those who dare question its validity. Generations of young men attended the school to carry on the family tradition of excellence where futures are charted and shaped by family expectations.

Enter John Keating, played by the late Robin Williams, a former student and alumni of Welton Academy. As a young man, he was a member of the Dead Poets Society, a group of students who would sneak off to read poetry and fantasies. In the opening scene, Mr. Keating led his classroom into the famed hallway of Welton Academy. This held trophy cases and pictures of those who had come before. They had been immortalized and were to be revered.

Into this setting and atmosphere, the line Carpe Diem was uttered, meaning "Seize the Day." I can hear Mr. Keating urging his students to lean in and hear the immortalized pictures speak. As they inched closer, Mr. Keating whispered over and over again, Carpe diem, seize the day!

One student cannot see hope when his dreams of being an actor are overridden by his father. After the dismissal of Mr. Keating for teaching principles outside of Welton traditions, several young men stand on their desks. They cry out, "O captain, my captain" in defiance to the school headmaster and in honor of their teacher.

"Seize the day, boys. Make your lives extraordinary!"
Dead Poets Society

There are a few takeaway moments we can apply as we consider "going."

Jesus invites us not to go for
Him, but to go with Him!

Mr. Keating speaks truth when he says, "We are food for worms lads." One day we will all die. Will our lives have mattered? Not hallowed in a trophy case, but engraved in the heart and soul of others?

And as it is appointed for men to die once, but after this the judgment.

Hebrews 9:27

Sometimes, I think about an alternate ending where the script could have moved from the poetry of men to the poetry of scripture and offered wisdom. When this knowledge is attained, it lasts for eternity. When the student saw no hope, it would have been wonderful for him to have read these words of Jesus.

The thief does not come except to steal, and to kill, and to destroy. I have come that they may have life, and that they may have it more abundantly.

John 10:10

As you pray about your role in His adventure, "Seize the Day!" Missions are multi-generational! Listen to one final line from the movie that Mr. Keating shares with a student who was nearly dismissed from the school.

"There's a time for daring and there's a time for caution and a wise man understands which is called for."

Dead Poets Society

Jesus is calling you to accept your role, assignment, and place in His expedition. We played the role of caution for too long. Seize the day!

See then that you walk circumspectly, not as fools but as wise, redeeming the time, because the days are evil. Therefore do not be unwise, but understand what the will of the Lord is.

Ephesians 5:15–17

DAY 26

God's Voice

John's gospel describes John the Baptist as simple and straightforward. He was a member of the human race, with a divine call. In Mark's gospel, the Romans are his target audience, where he uniquely presents Jesus as a humble servant. In introducing John the Baptist, he focuses on the servant aspect of the kingdom. At the time of the gospel of Mark, seventy percent of Rome were said to be slaves.

There was a man sent from God, whose name was John.

John 1:6

Mark's work includes some of the finer details about John's life and calling: his purpose, proclamation, platform, presentation, and preaching.

His Purpose: Deliver a message that had been personally given to him by Jesus Christ in the wilderness.

John was, as scripture describes him, "a voice." One thing that fascinates me about the faithfulness of God is that He always has a voice.

His Proclamation: A message of repentance, turning from sin unto God with a public profession of faith through water baptism. John challenged anyone who would repent of their sins to join him in the Jordan River. In other words, if you got right with God at one of John's services, you went home wet!

His Platform: The wilderness. John's missional journey wouldn't be found in a church planting manual. His audience was the rejects of society and those on the run from the law. Within a few short months, the religious leaders were making the journey to the wilderness to find out where the people of the city were worshipping.

**The King is coming.
Prepare to meet the King!**

His Presentation: He dressed and ate differently than the people he was called to reach.

His Preaching: I'm not the King, but the King is coming. Mark described John's preaching as a message of humility. John proclaims he was the lowest form of a servant on the planet, who wasn't even worthy to take off the shoes of the Master. John became great because he allowed his voice to be used by the Master.

John was held in high esteem, but held himself as a lowly servant. As you follow Christ, follow this model of John as you seek to elevate Jesus.

DAY 27

Already Sent

We have been commissioned, by Christ, to tell those who do not know Jesus about a Savior who loves them and died for them.

Then, the same day at evening, being the first day of the week, when the doors were shut where the disciples were assembled, for fear of the Jews, Jesus came and stood in the midst, and said to them, "Peace be with you." When He had said this, He showed them His hands and His side. Then the disciples were glad when they saw the Lord.

So Jesus said to them again, "Peace to you! As the Father has sent Me, I also send you."

John 20:19-21

When a team leaves for a mission trip, we have a time of public commissioning and prayer. Our teams go through six months of training and preparation. We double-check to ensure our prayer partners are secured and all the necessary paperwork is in order. The team shares their two-minute testimonies numerous times, or they use a visual aid and presentation to share the gospel. They have had six months of devotions and team building, and receive their particular assignment for the trip.

During our public commissioning, we invite all team members to the altar and have their families and prayer partners gather to pray for safety, health, and unity. We pray for the team to accomplish their main objective to lift, support, and encourage the missionaries we are serving. We always go to help implement the vision of the missionary in the field. Our commissioning times are exciting, emotional, and Christ-centered.

Read Jesus' words again, "Peace to you! As the Father has sent me, I also send you." You may wonder where did Jesus commission His followers to go? The good news is that He has already answered that question.

As You sent Me into the world, I also have sent them into the world.

John 17:18

"The World!" Jesus boldly says to you and I, pick a spot on the map, and you will find that I am there. His Spirit is already working among the people so He can have a representative in heaven of every tribe, tongue, and people.

> *After these things I looked, and behold, a great multi-tude which no one could number, of all nations, tribes, peoples, and tongues, standing before the throne and before the Lamb, clothed with white robes, with palm branches in their hands, and crying out with a loud voice, saying, "Salvation belongs to our God who sits on the throne, and to the Lamb!"*
>
> *Revelation 7:9-10*

I find it incredible that He would trust us with this adventure. He does not send us alone or unprepared for spiritual warfare.

Both of my daughters traveled internationally, but my wife was the first to set foot on foreign soil to join a mission trip to Istanbul, Turkey. As we prayed over that first journey, I had a lump in my throat, knowing that our lives were getting ready to change. I knew this would not be our last trip, but what I did not know is that the second time I would pray for a team, it would be sending them to the same place. They were to be the hands and feet of Jesus as the nation had been devastated by an earthquake. That would change their travels significantly. The

The Father, The Son, and The Holy Spirit, in essence and unity, commission us to take the adventure with Them!

prayer walking, praying over parks, schools, and certain areas filled with ordinary people living happy lives turned to the sounds and smell of death everywhere. Allow Him to change you forever as you accept His commissioning to go. He has already sent you!

DAY 28

Strong Delusion

When Andrew and I traveled to Baire, Cuba, I was introduced to the host church by their Pastor, Victor. He had attended our Missions Conference and passionately shared the need in Eastern Cuba. The majority of missions in Cuba begin in Havana and then head out to the western side. Baire is a sixteen-hour drive from Havana, but when I heard Pastor Victor's passion for training pastors, I had to go!

> *He who believes in the Son has everlasting life; and he*
> *who does not believe the Son shall not see life, but the*
> *wrath of God abides on him.*
>
> *John 3:36*

Cultivating a passion for missions is found through scripture. As we study scripture, we get glimpses of what the reception of the gospel will look like as we approach the return of Jesus. Natural disasters, the breakdown of law and order in our cities, violence in our streets, and unchecked immorality that slaughters the innocent unborn and calls it a "choice" are symptoms of a nation in deep reversionism. Break down this scripture into phrases to meditate on.

> The coming of the lawless one is according to the working of Satan, with all power, signs, and lying wonders, and with all unrighteous deception among those who perish, because they did not receive the love of the truth, that they might be saved. And for this reason God will send them strong delusion, that they should believe the lie, that they all may be condemned who did not believe the truth but had pleasure in unrighteousness.
>
> *2 Thessalonians 2:9-12*

This scripture says the "spirit of antichrist" is already here. The culmination of this passage will reach its peak fulfillment in the Tribulation. But, strong delusion has already taken a firm hold on America and the world.

Satan is alive and well, and the forces of darkness do not slumber. Unrighteous deception fills the pulpits of America and deceives those "who perish." It is not that people did not comprehend the truth, but they "did not receive the love of the truth, that they might be saved."

"Spend a lifetime telling God to be quiet, and He will do just that. In hell, God honors our request for silence. Hell is not a correctional facility or reform school. Its members hear no candid sermons. They do not hear the Spirit of God, or the voice of God, or the voice of God's people."

Max Lucado, 3:16

One of the saddest statements in the Bible is when God says Sir, Ma'am, if that's your desire, I will honor your choice. We are dangerously close to those verses coming to fruition to those who have "pleasure in unrighteousness." Join His adventure while there is still time to share, and the gospel can be received.

DAY 29

The Process

Then Jesus went about all the cities and villages, teach-
ing in their synagogues, preaching the gospel of the
kingdom, and healing every sickness and every disease
among the people. But when He saw the multitudes,
He was moved with compassion for them, because they
were weary and scattered, like sheep having no shep-
herd. Then He said to His disciples, "The harvest truly
is plentiful, but the laborers are few. Therefore pray
the Lord of the harvest to send out laborers into His
harvest."

Mathew 9:35-38

Y ou don't have to find God's will for your life; it isn't lost. We have the Bible as our guide and Jesus as our instructor.

The former account I made, O Theophilus, of all that Jesus began both to do and teach, until the day in which He was taken up, after He through the Holy Spirit had given commandments to the apostles whom He had chosen, to whom He also presented Himself alive after His suffering by many infallible proofs, being seen by them during forty days and speaking of the things pertaining to the kingdom of God.

Acts 1:1-3

In the Greek language, when two infinitives are placed together, the second is the stronger emphasized. Jesus' teachings live on today and are still changing lives. Every miracle in the Bible has a message. Miracles do not happen every day. If they did, they would not be called miracles, just occurrences. The teachings of Jesus are offensive to some, a stumbling-block on their journey. To others, they are the power of God unto salvation.

In Matthew 9:35, the Bible says Jesus *went*. Jesus left the building and went into the cities and villages. He left the temple, the small group, and the church. He left the comfortable surroundings of Nazareth and went to places He had never been before.

Verse 36 gives the next clue; He *saw*. He saw the multitudes. How do you navigate the multitudes? One person at a time, making eye contact to focus on people, not crowds. Jesus was *moved* by what He saw.

He was moved with *compassion*. They were weary and scattered. He uses the metaphor of a sheep with no shepherd, a sitting duck for the enemy.

Then Jesus *prayed*. Do not get the process of Jesus out-of-order. He went, He saw, He was moved, and then He prayed. Many challenged to join Him, and give a spiritual answer, which says, "I'll pray about it." That is code for "I'm not doing anything!"

He instructed His disciples to pray to the Lord of the harvest. What were they to pray? Lord, *send out* laborers into His harvest. Notice that it is *"His"* harvest, and remember, we are given the gift to join Him.

You and I will never be moved until we walk amongst the people and see their needs.

Jesus then *called* in Matthew 10:1. He gave *power*, and in verse five, He *sent* the disciples on their first short-term mission trip.

There is always a moment in life when the door opens and lets in the future. Enjoy this moment. Destiny does not make appointments; it shows up at the door unannounced!

DAY 30

The Definition of Adventure

Here is the missional adventure we've been talking about for the last 30 days. You can define it or let it define you!

Noun: an unusual and exciting, typically hazardous, experience or activity; daring and exciting activity calling for enterprise and enthusiasm.

Verb: engage in a hazardous and exciting activity, especially the exploration of unknown territory; put (something, especially money or one's life) at risk.

"Faith is a verb; you don't own it. You live it!"

Jeff Christopherson

The funny thing that is running through my head is not the exciting, hazardous activity of the mission adventure itself. It's the daring exploration of the unknown in missions or life. So many people tell me they **"Faith is a verb; you don't own it. You live it!" Jeff Christopherson** don't go on mission trips because of the unknown dangers involved. You can live in the known and still have dangers surrounding you.

Make the word adventure in your life a verb, not a noun. It's something you do, and it defines you. Allow the words of Paul to guide you as you pray about your role in missions.

> *Therefore we do not lose heart. Even though our outward man is perishing, yet the inward man is being renewed day by day. For our light affliction, which is but for a moment, is working for us a far more exceeding and eternal weight of glory, while we do not look at the things which are seen, but at the things which are not seen. For the things which are seen are temporary, but the things which are not seen are eternal.*
>
> *2 Corinthians 4:16–18*

My adventure with missions began pulling a little red wagon. It continued at a Children's Home in Sevierville, TN, and has taken me to Africa, Cuba, Australia, and beyond. My prayer is that you will let go of the fears that keep you from being set free. Set free to allow the fruits the Holy Spirit will produce through you, and free to the empowering presence and anointing of the Holy Spirit.

> *The anointing of the Holy Spirit is a special touch for a special task.*
>
> *Dr. Stephen Olford*

Notes

Christopherson, J. (2019). Why a Leader's Character is More Important than Anything Else. *The Exchange*.

Greear, J. (2016, October 5). *We Judge Our Success by Sending Capacity, Not Seating Capacity*. Speech.

Hillis, D. (1977). *Missions Today*. Moody Bible Institute.

Lucado, M. (2007). *3:16*. Nashville, TN: Thomas Nelson.

Olford, S., Dr. *Successful Soul-Winning*. B&H Books.

Phillips, J., & Klingbell, H. E. (n.d.). *Teaching With Results*. Moody Bible Institute.

Polhill, J. B. (1992). *The New American commentary*. Nashville, TN: Broadman Press.

Weir, P. (Director). (1989). *Dead Poets Society (motion picture)* [Motion picture]. United States: Buena Vista Pictures Distribution.

Acknowledgments

Rick Busick and Mark Daubenmire – Thank you for joining the vision of reaching men and women for Jesus Christ, through hosting an annual golf tournament. Who would have ever dreamed that our small golf scramble would evolve to 96 players each year? The vision we adopted was to have an incredible outing to share the gospel and raise funds for missionaries locally, nationally, and around the world. Over twenty years later, having raised over one hundred thousand dollars and seeing 127 golfers find Jesus as Lord and Savior, I would like to say a "heart felt" thank you to you both. Whenever a soul is reached through You-Turn ministries, a Child's Hope International, and Caring Partners, we help play a role. It's an honor to not only be your pastor, but also to call you my friends.

Larry Conger – Thank you for donating a one week stay in Hilton Head every year as the grand prize drawing for our golf tournament. We've also enjoyed (maybe endured) five different building projects together at Urbancrest and currently our sixth project, an outdoor pavilion. Souls will continue to be added to His kingdom because of your giftedness.

Check out more resources at:
tompendergrass.org
www.urbancrest.org

CPSIA information can be obtained
at www.ICGtesting.com
Printed in the USA
BVHW060850150121
597916BV00004B/14